Acknowledgments

Joseph and Lois Bird (7), James Dobson (8,21,86,136,138,148), H. Norman Wright (16), Mother Teresa (17), Joseph Joubert (19), Dan Bennett (20), Margaret Fuller (24), Mae West (25), Charles Meigs (27), Richard Dobbins (28), Margaret E. Sangster (34), Thomas Kempis (35), Martin Luther (36, 93), Alvin Vander Griend (37), Ruth Bell Graham (38), George Adams (40), Winston Churchill (42), Glen Wheeler (45), Ogden Nash (47), Grit (49), Renee Jordan (53), Lady Bird Johnson (55), Mignon McLaughlin (62), Wilfred A. Peterson (63,139), Bishop Jeremy Taylor (64), Franklin P. Jones (66), Lucretius (68), Katherine Ann Porter (72), Ignacy Paderewski (73), Heine (74), Henry Longfellow (77), Andre Maurois (78), Louis Fromm (80), James Thurber (81), Hazel Scot (83), Maria Lovell (84), George Eliot

(87), R. A. Heinlein (90), Dennis Rainey (95), Peter Devries (96), Samuel Rogers (97), David Ingles (98), Robert W. Burns (100), Howard and Jeanne Hendricks (108), Jerry McCant (112), Joseph Addison (115), G. K. Chesterton (116), Doris Day (117), Mary Kay Ash (119,141), Konrad Adenauer (120), Thomas Fuller (121), Neil Warren (123), Benjamin Franklin (125), Paul E. Tsongas (126), John D. MacDonald (132), Peter Marshall (133), Betty Mills (134), Kin Hubbard (142), Balzac (143), Michael Green (145), Henry Longfellow (147), Harold S. Hulbert (149), M. Shain (150).

God's Little Instruction Book
for Couples

Honor Books, Inc.
P. O. Box 55388
Tulsa, OK 74155

12th Printing

God's Little Instruction Book
for Couples
ISBN 1-56292-102-9
Copyright © 1995 by Honor Books, Inc.
P. O. Box 55388
Tulsa, Oklahoma 74155

Introduction

God's Little Instruction Book for Couples is an inspirational collection of quotes and Scriptures that will motivate married couples to develop a meaningful, productive and happy life together while inspiring them to strive for excellence and character in living.

Appealing to couples of all ages, this little book is power packed with dynamic quotes on how to have a meaningful relationship.

This little book is designed to be fun to read, yet thought-provoking, supplying couples with godly insight on numerous topics vital to married life. An inspirational verse is included after each quote, so you can read what the instruction manual of life, the Bible, has to say about that topic.

God's Little Instruction Book for Couples will help couples to reach for excellence as they meet the challenges of their marriage and life together.

The family begins in a commitment of love.

For this reason a man shall leave his father and his mother and shall be joined to his wife, and the two shall become one flesh.
Ephesians 5:31 AMP

A personal relationship with Jesus Christ is the cornerstone of marriage.

Behold I lay in Zion a choice stone, a precious corner stone,
and he who believes in Him shall not be disappointed.
1 Peter 2:6b NAS

The most important thing a father can do for his children is to love their mother.

Husbands, love your wives, as Christ loved the church and gave Himself up for her.
Ephesians 5:25 AMP

Love is being willing to face risks to see your spouse's dreams come true.

This is how we know what love is: Jesus Christ laid down his life for us.
And we ought to lay down our lives for our brothers.
1 John 3:16 NIV

Nothing beats love at first sight except love with insight.

The beginning of wisdom is this: get wisdom,
and whatever you get, get insight.
Proverbs 4:7 RSV

The measure of a man is not how great his faith is but how great his love is.

Greater love has no man than this,
that a man lay down his life for his friends.
John 15:13 RSV

Advice to the wife:
Be to his virtues very kind.
Be to his faults a little blind.

[Love] is not easily angered, it keeps no record of wrongs . . .
but rejoices with the truth.
1 Corinthians 13:5,6 NIV

Before marriage the three little words are, "I love you." After marriage they are, "Let's eat out."

But he that is married careth for the things that are of the world, how he may please his wife.
1 Corinthians 7:33

A house is made of walls and beams; a home is made of love and dreams.

She looks well to the ways of her household,
and does not eat the bread of idleness.
Proverbs 31:27 NAS

The direction of your
thought life can determine
the course of your marriage.

Keep thy heart with all diligence; for out of it are the issues of life.
Proverbs 4:23

Kind words can be short and easy to speak, but their echoes are truly endless.

Pleasant words are as an honeycomb,
sweet to the soul, and health to the bones.
Proverbs 16:24

A loving spouse can see the good in you even when you can't.

*Be patient with each other, making allowance
for each other's faults because of your love.*
Ephesians 4:2b TLB

Children have more need of models than of critics.

Be their ideal; let them follow the way you teach and live; be a pattern for them in your love, your faith, and your clean thoughts.
1 Timothy 4:12 TLB

An argument is the longest distance between two points.

When angry, do not sin; do not ever let your wrath (your exasperation, your fury or indignation) last until the sun goes down.
Ephesians 4:26 AMP

It is our uniqueness that gives freshness and vitality to a relationship.

For I am fearfully and wonderfully made.
Psalms 139:14b

Give your troubles to God; He will be up all night anyway.

. . . casting all your anxiety upon Him, because He cares for you.
1 Peter 5:7 NAS

Our prayer life never needs a bridle, but sometimes it needs a spur.

Is any one of you in trouble? He should pray.
James 5:13a,b NIV

Men for the sake of getting a living forget to live.

So don't worry at all about having enough food and clothing.
Why be like the heathen? For they take pride in all these things
and are deeply concerned about them. But your heavenly
Father already knows perfectly well that you need them.
Matthew 6:31 TLB

The best way to hold a man is in your arms.

May your unfailing love be my comfort,
according to your promise to your servant.
Psalm 119:76 NIV

The best way for you and
your spouse to guarantee
some time without the kids is
to do the dinner dishes together.

*Two can accomplish more than twice as much
as one, for the results can be much better.*
Ecclesiastes 4:9 TLB

What is a home without a Bible?
'Tis a home where daily bread
for the body is provided,
but the soul is never fed.

. . . it is written, "Man shall not live by bread alone,
but by every word that proceeds from the mouth of God."
Matthew 4:4 RSV

The closer a man and his wife get to Christ, the clearer they see how important it is for them to stay close to each other.

And though a man might prevail against one who is alone, two will withstand him. A threefold cord is not quickly broken.
Ecclesiastes 4:12 RSV

Children are natural mimics –
they act like their parents
in spite of every attempt to
teach them good manners.

I have set you an example that you should do as I have done for you.
John 13:15 NIV

Love makes a house a home.

You will be happy and it will be well with you.
Your wife shall be like a fruitful vine, within your house,
your children like olive plants around your table.
Psalms 128:2b,3 NAS

You will never "find" time
for anything. If you want
time you must make it.

Whatever your hand finds to do, do it with all your might.
Ecclesiastes 9:10a NIV

The kind of music people should have in their homes is domestic harmony.

And above all these put on love, which
binds everything together in perfect harmony.
Colossians 3:14 RSV

Ninety percent of the friction of daily life is caused by the wrong tone of voice.

A man finds joy in giving an apt reply – and how good is a timely word!
Proverbs 15:23 NIV

Marriage must exemplify friendship's highest ideal, or else it will be a failure.

And here is how to mearusre it — the greatest love is shown when a person lays down his life for his friends.
John 15:13 TLB

A wise lover values not so much the gift of the lover as the love of the giver.

How fair is thy love, my sister, my spouse! how much better is thy love than wine! and the smell of thine ointments than all spices!
Song of Solomon 4:10

There is no more lovely, friendly and charming relationship, communion or company than a good marriage.

A wife of noble character is her husband's crown.
Proverbs 12:4 NIV

You can do everything else right as a parent, but if you don't begin with loving God, you're going to fail.

But as for me and my house, we will serve the Lord.
Joshua 24:15b RSV

A happy marriage is the union of two good forgivers.

And be kind to one another, tenderhearted, forgiving one another, just as God in Christ also forgave you.
Ephesians 4:32 NKJV

Forgiveness is giving love when there is no reason to . . .

Blessed are the merciful, for they shall obtain mercy.
Matthew 5:7 NKJV

We should seize every opportunity to give encouragement. Encouragement is oxygen to the soul.

But encourage one another daily, as long as it is called Today . . .
Hebrews 3:13 NIV

You can create an oasis of love in the midst of a harsh and uncaring world by grinding it out and sticking in there.

A new command I give you: Love one another.
As I have loved you, so you must love one another.
John 13:34 NIV

My most brilliant achievement was to be able to persuade my wife to marry me.

To everything there is a season: A time to get....
Ecclesiastes 3:1,6

The bonds of matrimony are worthless unless the interest is kept up.

Live happily with the woman you love through the fleeting days of life, for the wife God gives you is your best reward down here for all your earthly toil.
Ecclesiastes 9:9 TLB

Marriage may be inspired by
music, soft words, and perfume;
but its security is manifest
in work, consideration,
respect, and well-fried bacon.

*Nevertheless let each one of you in particular so love his own wife
as himself, and let the wife see that she respects her husband.*
Ephesians 5:33 NKJV

Many parents are finding out
that a pat on the back helps
develop character –
if given often enough,
early enough, and low enough.

Correct your son, and he will give you rest;
Yes, he will give delight to your soul.
Proverbs 29:17 NKJV

The great thing about being married a long time is falling in love with the same person again . . . and again . . . and again.

Let thy fountain be blessed: and rejoice with the wife of thy youth . . .
and be thou ravished always with her love.
Proverbs 5:18,19c

To keep your marriage brimming, with love in the loving cup, whenever you're wrong, admit it, whenever you're right, shut up.

Confess to one another therefore your faults . . . and pray [also] for one another, that you may be healed and restored . . .
James 5:16a AMP

A marriage may be made in heaven, but the maintenance must be done on earth.

Practice what you have learned and received and heard and seen in me, and model your way of living on it, and the God of peace (of untroubled, undisturbed well-being) will be with you.
Philippians 4:9 AMP

The most impressive example of tolerance is a golden wedding anniversary.

Let your fountain (of human life) be blessed (with the rewards of fidelity), and rejoice in the wife of your youth.
Proverbs 5:18 AMP

The best things to get out of marriage are children.

Behold, children are a gift of the Lord; The fruit of the womb is a reward.
Psalm 127:3 NAS

First secure an independent income, then practice virtue.

Finish your outdoor work and get your fields ready;
after that, build your house.
Proverbs 24:27 NIV

How to be a happily married couple can never really be taught, only learned.

And try to learn (in your experience) what is pleasing to the Lord let your lives be constant proofs of what is most acceptable to Him.
Ephesians 5:10 AMP

We need to be patient with
our children in the same
way God is patient with us.

And, fathers, do not provoke your children to anger;
but bring them up in the discipline and instruction of the Lord.
Ephesians 6:4 NAS

Nothing is so strong as gentleness. Nothing is so gentle as real strength.

Thou hast also given me the shield of Thy salvation, And Thy right hand upholds me; And Thy gentleness makes me great.
Psalm 18:35 NAS

If we must disagree, let's disagree without being disagreeable.

. . . as far as it depends on you, live at peace with everyone.
Romans 12:18 AMP

Marriage is a marathon, not a sprint.

And Jacob served seven years for Rachel; and they seemed unto
him but a few days, for the love he had to her.
Genesis 29:20

Sharing the housework makes it easier to share the love.

Bear one another's burdens, and so fulfill the law of Christ.
Galatians 6:2 RSV

Don't take yourself too seriously, but never fail to take your spouse seriously.

Do nothing from selfishness or empty conceit, but with humility of mind let each of you regard one another as more important than himself.
Philippians 2:3 NAS

No marriage is all sunshine,
but two people can share one
umbrella if they huddle close.

... if two lie down together, then they have warmth;
but how can one be warm alone?
Ecclesiastes 4:11 AMP

Good listeners make good lovers.

Listen to advice and accept instruction, and in the end you will be wise.
Proverbs 19:20 NIV

It takes two to make a quarrel.

A soft answer turns away wrath, But a harsh word stirs up anger.
Proverbs 15:1 NKJV

A successful marriage requires falling in love many times, always with the same person.

I will betroth you to me forever; I will betroth you in righteousness and justice, in love and compassion.
Hosea 2:19 NIV

In practicing the art of
parenthood an ounce of
example is worth a ton
of preachment.

Therefore be imitators of God, as beloved children . . .
Ephesians 5:1 NAS

Love is friendship set on fire.

Many waters cannot quench love, neither can floods drown it.
Song of Solomon 8:7 RSV

Best friends make the best spouses.

There is a friend that sticketh closer than a brother.
Proverbs 18:24b

Love doesn't make the world go 'round. Love is what makes the ride worthwhile.

There are three things that remain — faith, hope, and love —
and the greatest of these is love.
1 Corinthians 13:13 TLB

Lay aside life-harming heaviness and entertain a cheerful disposition.

A glad heart makes a cheerful countenance,
but by sorrow of heart the spirit is broken.
Proverbs 15:13 AMP

Love is a product of habit.

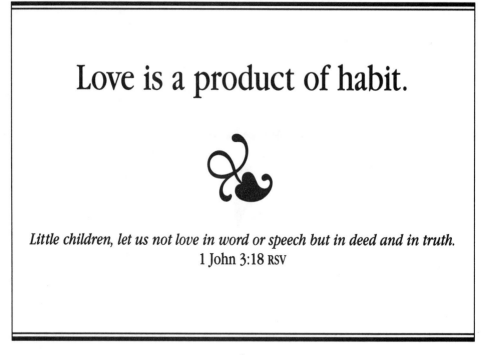

Little children, let us not love in word or speech but in deed and in truth.
1 John 3:18 RSV

After winning an argument with his wife, the wisest thing a man can do is apologize.

In the same way you married men should live considerately with [your wives], with an intelligent recognition [of the marriage relation], honoring the woman . . .
1 Peter 3:7a AMP

Love's lasting comes in erasing the boundary line between "mine" and "yours."

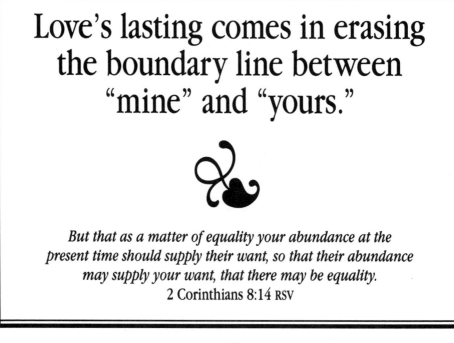

But that as a matter of equality your abundance at the present time should supply their want, so that their abundance may supply your want, that there may be equality.
2 Corinthians 8:14 RSV

Children don't divide a couple's love – they multiply it.

Children are a gift from God; they are his reward.
Psalm 127:3 TLB

Love must be learned, and learned again and again; there is no end to it.

And this I pray, that your love may abound yet more and more in knowledge and in all judgment.
Philippians 1:9

Everyone has patience.
Successful people learn to use it.

But let patience have her perfect work, that ye may be perfect and entire, wanting nothing.
James 1:4

Matrimony – the high sea for which no compass has yet been invented.

There are three things too wonderful for me to understand –
no four! . . . How a ship finds its way across the heaving ocean.
The growth of love between a man and a girl.
Proverbs 30:18 TLB

Marriage is not for wimps.

Let marriage be held in honor (esteemed worthy, precious, of great price and especially dear) in all things. And thus let the marriage bed be undefiled . . . for God will judge . . . [all guilty of sexual vice] . . .
Hebrews 13:4 AMP

A joyful marriage is a bit of heaven on earth.

Enjoy life with the woman whom you love all the days
of your fleeting life which He has given to
you under the sun; for this is your reward in life . . .
Ecclesiastes 9:9 NAS

Love gives itself; it is not bought.

Many waters cannot quench love, Nor will rivers overflow it;
If a man were to give all the riches of his house for love,
It would be utterly despised.
Song of Solomon 8:7 NAS

A happy marriage is a long conversation which always seems too short.

Let the words of my mouth, and the meditation
of my heart, be acceptable in thy sight, O Lord . . .
Psalm 19:14

Two can live as cheaply as one — if one doesn't eat.

There is a right time for everything: A time to laugh....
Ecclesiastes 3:1,4 TLB

Straighten your problems out before you go to bed. That way you will wake up smiling.

Be angry, and yet do not sin; do not let the sun go down on your anger . . .
Ephesians 4:26 NAS

Love is what you've been through with somebody.

It (love) always protects, always trusts, always hopes, always perseveres.
1 Corinthians 13:7 NIV

Marriage is a promise that
is shared by only two – a vow
to love and dream and plan
together all life through.

*... if two of you on earth agree (harmonize together,
make a symphony together) about whatever [anything and
everything] they may ask, it will come to pass and be done for them ...*
Matthew 18:19 AMP

There's a time when you have to explain to your children why they're born, and it's a marvelous thing if you know the reason.

Before I [God] formed thee in the belly I knew thee; and before thou camest forth out of the womb I sanctified thee, and I ordained thee . . . .
Jeremiah 1:5

Two souls with but a single thought, two hearts that beat as one.

. . . a man shall leave his father and mother and be joined to his wife, and the two shall become one flesh.
Ephesians 5:31 NKJV

Spouses who put their partners first have marriages that last.

. . . but in lowliness of mind let each esteem other better than themselves.
Philippians 2:3b

Successful marriages usually rest on a foundation of accountability between husbands and wives.

Submitting yourselves one to another in the fear of God.
Ephesians 5:21

What greater thing is there
for two human souls than to
feel that they are joined for life.

What therefore God hath joined together, let no man put asunder.
Matthew 19:6b

Be careful that your marriage doesn't become a duel instead of a duet.

Let us therefore follow after the things which make for peace, and things wherewith one may edify another.
Romans 14:19

You can send your marriage to an early grave with a series of little digs.

Death and life are in the power of the tongue:
and they that love it shall eat the fruit thereof.
Proverbs 18:21

Love is the condition in which
the happiness of another person
is essential to your own.

[Love] . . . does not seek its own.
1 Corinthians 13:5b NAS

Being married teaches us at least one very valuable lesson – to think before we speak.

A word aptly spoken is like apples of gold in settings of silver.
Proverbs 25:11 NIV

A good marriage is . . .
a relationship where a healthy
perspective overlooks a
multitude of "unresolvables".

*Above all, love each other deeply, because love
covers over a multitude of sins.*
1 Peter 4:8 NIV

Let the wife make the husband glad to come home, and let him make her sorry to see him leave.

...let each man of you (without exception) love his wife as (being in a sense) his very own self; and let the wife see that she respects and reveres her husband (that she notices him, regards him...).
Ephesians 5:33 AMP

Watch out for temptation –
the more you see of it
the better it looks.

Keep watching and praying, that you may not come into temptation...
Mark 14:38a NAS

Forgiveness means giving up your right to punish another.

And when you stand praying, if you hold anything against anyone, forgive him, so that your Father in heaven may forgive you your sins.
Mark 11:25 NIV

The difficulty with marriage
is that we fall in love with
a personality, but must live
with a character.

Confess your faults one to another, and pray one for another . . . .
James 5:16a

It doesn't matter who you marry, for you are sure to find out the next morning that it was someone else.

I will betroth you to me in faithfulness and love, and you will really know me then as you never have before.
Hosea 2:20 TLB

Love is giving more and never keeping score.

[Love] takes no account of the evil done to it
[it pays no attention to a suffered wrong].
1 Corinthians 13:5d AMP

The best comforter isn't a down-filled quilt.

Even though I walk through the valley of the shadow of death, I fear no evil; for Thou art with me; Thy rod and Thy staff, they comfort me.
Psalm 23:4 NAS

No man or woman is a failure
who has helped hold happily
a home together. He who has
been victorious in his home can
never be completely defeated.

*Blessed is the man whose quiver is full of them; they shall not be
ashamed, When they speak with their enemies in the gate.*
Psalm 127:5 NAS

The key to a healthy marriage
is to keep your eyes wide
open before you wed . . .
and half closed thereafter.

And be kind to one another, tenderhearted, forgiving one another,
just as God in Christ also forgave you.
Ephesians 4:32 NKJV

Making marriage work is like operating a farm. You have to start all over again each morning.

*Cause me to hear Your lovingkindness
in the morning, For in You do I trust.*
Psalm 143:8a NKJV

Married couples who claim they have never had an argument in forty years either have poor memories or a very dull life to recall.

Faithful are the wounds of a friend, but the kisses of an enemy are lavish and deceitful.
Proverbs 27:6 AMP

Service is nothing but love in work clothes.

The more lowly your service to others, the greater
you are. To be the greatest, be a servant.
Matthew 23:11 TLB

You keep a lifetime commitment by keeping promises day by day.

But let your statement be, "Yes, yes" or "No, no";
and anything beyond these is of evil.
Matthew 5:37 NAS

Remember: The course of true love is full of obstacles.

For you have need of endurance, so that after you have done the will of God, you may receive the promise.
Hebrews 10:36 NKJV

It is such a comfort to drop the tangles of life into God's hands and leave them there.

Cast your cares on the Lord and he will sustain you.
Psalm 55:22 NIV

The difference between
smooth sailing and shipwreck
in marriage lies in what you
as a couple are doing about
the rough weather.

If thou faint in the day of adversity, thy strength is small.
Proverbs 24:10

Married life is a marathon. It is not enough to make a great start toward a long-term marriage. You need determination . . .

You need to keep on patiently doing God's will if you want him to do for you all that he has promised.
Hebrews 10:36 TLB

Real joy comes not from riches or from the praise of men but from doing something worthwhile.

It is more blessed to give than to receive.
Acts 20:35b NIV

Courtesy costs nothing, yet it buys things that are priceless.

To sum up, let all be harmonious, sympathetic,
brotherly, kindhearted, and humble in spirit.
1 Peter 3:8 NAS

You can never be happily married to another until you get a divorce from yourself. Successful marriage demands a certain death to self.

And they that are Christ's have crucified the flesh with the affections and lusts. If we live in the Spirit, let us also walk in the Spirit.
Galatians 5:24,25

Love is the one business in which it pays to be an absolute spendthrift: Give it away; throw it away; splash it over; empty your pockets; shake the basket; and tomorrow you'll have more than ever.

Give, and it will be given to you. A good measure, pressed down, shaken together and running over, will be poured into your lap. For with the measure you use, it will be measured to you.
Luke 6:38 NIV

Superfluous wealth can
buy superfluities only.
Money is not required to buy
one necessity of the soul.

Wealth is worthless in the day of wrath,
but righteousness delivers from death.
Proverbs 11:4 NIV

Friendship improves happiness, and abates misery, by doubling our joy, and dividing our grief.

A friend loves at all times, and a brother is born for adversity.
Proverbs 17:17 NIV

Love means to love that which is
unlovable, or it is no virtue at all:
Forgiving means to pardon
that which is unpardonable,
or it is no virtue at all.

*Be gentle and forbearing wtih one another and, if one has a difference (a
grievance or complaint) against another, readily pardoning each other;
even as the Lord has (freely) forgiven you, so must you also (forgive).*
Colossians 3:13 AMP

If the husband and wife can possibly afford it, they should definitely have separate bathrooms for the sake of their marriage.

A happy heart is good medicine and a cheerful mind works healing....
Proverbs 17:22 AMP

A good husband should be deaf and a good wife should be blind.

Be gentle and ready to forgive; never hold grudges..
Colossians 3:13a TLB

Everyone has an invisible sign hanging from his neck saying, "Make me feel important!"

Therefore encourage one another and build each other up, just as in fact you are doing.
1 Thessalonians 5:11 NIV

A thick skin is a gift from God.

A man's wisdom gives him patience;
it is to his glory to overlook an offense.
Proverbs 19:11 NIV

All things are difficult before they are easy.

Blessed is the man who perseveres under trial,
because when he has stood the test, he will receive the
crown of life that God has promised to those who love him.
James 1:12 NIV

Marriage is like harmony: two sets of notes for the same song.

*Complete my joy by being of the same mind, having
the same love, being in full accord and of one mind.*
Philippians 2:2 RSV

Intimacy is the mystical bond of friendship, commitment, and understanding.

. . . there is a friend who sticks closer than a brother.
Proverbs 18:24b AMP

If love is a jigsaw puzzle, falling in love is finding the corners.

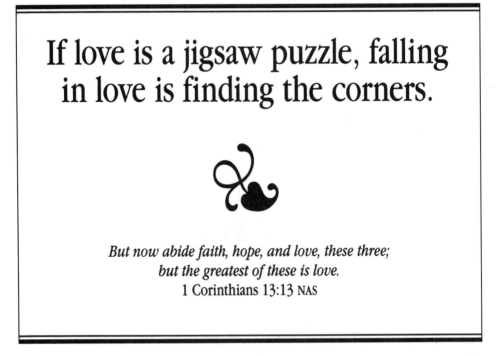

But now abide faith, hope, and love, these three;
but the greatest of these is love.
1 Corinthians 13:13 NAS

If you would be wealthy, think of saving as well as getting.

The ants are a people not strong, yet they lay up their food in the summer.
Proverbs 30:25 AMP

No one on his deathbed ever said "I wish I had spent more time on my business."

Do not labor for the food which perishes,
but for the food which endures to eternal life . . .
John 6:27a RSV

May the love you share be
as timeless as the tides
and as deep as the sea.

Love never ends . . .
1 Corinthians 13:8a RSV

My wife is very punctual. In fact, she buys everything on time.

The heart of her husband doth safely trust in her,
so that he shall have no need of spoil.
Proverbs 31:11

God gave women a sense of humor – so they could understand the jokes they married.

A merry heart doeth good like a medicine.
Proverbs 17:22a

Lean on each other's strengths; forgive each other's weaknesses.

Bearing with one another, and forgiving one other.
Colossians 3:13a NKJV

Never, never, be too proud to say "I'm sorry" to your child when you've made a mistake.

Fathers, do not irritate and provoke your children to anger [do not exasperate them to resentment], but rear them [tenderly] in the . . . discipline and the counsel . . . of the Lord.
Ephesians 6:4 AMP

Friendships, like marriages, are dependent on avoiding the unforgivable.

Be kind and compassionate to one another,
forgiving each other, just as in Christ God forgave you.
Ephesians 4:32 NIV

You cannot do a kindness too soon, because you never know how soon it will be too late!

But encourage one another day after day,
as long as it is still called "Today"...
Hebrews 3:13 NAS

Daily prayers will diminish your cares.

Have no anxiety about anything, but in everything by prayer and supplication with thanksgiving let your requests be made known to God.
Philippians 4:6 RSV

It is more important to get in the first thought than the last word.

But let everyone be quick to hear, slow to speak and slow to anger...
James 1:19 NAS

A husband should compliment his wife, bring her flowers and tell her that he cares. These are the ingredients of genuine passion.

Her children rise up and bless her; Her husband also, and he praises her, saying: "Many daughters have done nobly, But you excel them all."
Proverbs 31:28,29 NAS

Before criticizing your wife's faults,
you must remember it may have been
these very defects which prevented
her from getting a better husband
than the one she married.

Therefore let us not judge one another anymore, but rather determine
this — not to put an obstacle or a stumbling block in a brother's way.
Romans 14:13 NAS

The most successful marriages
are those where both the
husband and the wife seek to
build the self-esteem of the other.

Therefore encourage one another, and build up one another...
1 Thessalonians 5:11 NAS

Our children are watching us live, and what we are shouts louder than anything we can say.

. . . let us not love with word or with tongue, but in deed and truth.
1 John 3:18 NAS

The sunlight of love will kill all the germs of jealousy and hate.

Love never fails . . .
1 Corinthians 13:8a NAS

Stack every bit of criticism between two layers of praise.

Correct, rebuke and encourage –
with great patience and careful instruction.
2 Timothy 4:2c NIV

Of all the home remedies, a good wife is best.

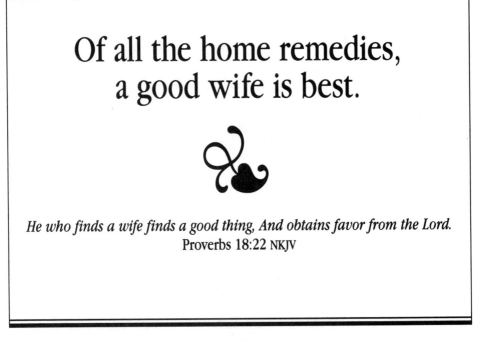

He who finds a wife finds a good thing, And obtains favor from the Lord.
Proverbs 18:22 NKJV

A woman must be a genius to create a good husband.

She opens her mouth in skillful and godly Wisdom,
and on her tongue is the law of kindness . . .
Proverbs 31:26 AMP

Success in marriage is more than finding the right person. It's also a matter of being the right person.

And just as you want people to treat you, treat them in the same way.
Luke 6:31 NAS

Unless loving your family is a high priority, you may gain the world and lose your children.

Fathers, do not provoke your children, lest they become discouraged.
Colossians 3:21 NKJV

The world needs more warm hearts and fewer hot heads.

Good sense makes a man slow to anger,
and it is his glory to overlook an offense.
Proverbs 19:11 RSV

A torn jacket is soon mended; but hard words bruise the heart of a child.

But I tell you that men will have to give account on the day of judgment for every careless word they have spoken.
Matthew 12:36 NIV

You have a lifetime to enjoy one another. Don't waste a day of it.

*Live happily with the woman you love through
the fleeting days of your life . . .*
Ecclesiastes 9:9a TLB

Children need love, especially when they do not deserve it.

. . . Let the children come to me, and do not hinder them, for the kingdom of heaven belongs to such as these.
Matthew 19:14 NIV

Loving can cost a lot, but not loving always costs more.

And if I give all my possessions to feed the poor, and if I deliver my body to be burned, but do not have love, it profits me nothing.
1 Corinthians 13:3 NAS

In trying times, don't quit trying.

*And let us not grow weary in well-doing, for in due season
we shall reap, if we do not lose heart.*
Galatians 6:9 RSV

Friendship is the marriage of the soul.

Two are better than one, because they have a good return for their work.
Ecclesiastes 4:9 NIV

People in love want what's best for each other.

Love bears all things, believes all things,
hopes all things, endures all things.
1 Corinthians 13:7 RSV

Marriage takes commitment; all good things do.

So guard yourself in your spirit, and do not break faith with the wife of your youth.
Malachi 2:15c NIV

Hug therapy really works.

Love one another with brotherly affection ...
giving precedence and showing honor to one another.
Romans 12:10 AMP

When Adam was lonely, God created for him not ten friends, but one wife.

A wife of noble character who can find?
She is worth far more than rubies.
Proverbs 31:10 NIV

"Family" was God's idea and He does not make mistakes.

For this cause a man shall leave his father and his mother, and shall cleave to his wife; and they shall become one flesh.
Genesis 2:24 NAS

References

Unless otherwise indicated, all Scripture quotations are taken from the *King James Version* of the Bible.

Scripture quotations marked AMP are taken from *The Amplified Bible. Old Testament* copyright © 1965, 1987 by Zondervan Corporation. New Testament copyright © 1958, 1987 by the Lockman Foundation. Used by permission.

Scripture quotations marked NAS are taken from the *New American Standard Bible.* Copyright © The Lockman Foundation 1960, 1962, 1963, 1968, 1971, 1972, 1973, 1975, 1977. Used by permission.

Scripture quotations marked NIV are taken from the *Holy Bible: New International Version.* Copyright © 1973, 1978, 1984 by International Bible Society. Used by permission of Zondervan Bible Publishers.

Scripture quotations marked NKJV are taken from *The New King James Version* of the Bible. Copyright © 1979, 1980, 1982 by Thomas Nelson, Inc., Publishers. Used by permission.

Verses marked TLB are taken from *The Living Bible,* copyright © 1971. Used by permission of Tyndale House Publishers, Inc., Wheaton, Illinois 60189. All rights reserved.

Scripture quotations marked RSV are taken from *The Revised Standard Version of the Bible,* copyright © 1946, Old Testament section copyright © 1952 by the Division of Christian Education of the Churches of Christ in the United States of America and is used by permission.

Additional copies of this book and other titles
in the *God's Little Instruction Book* series
are available at your local bookstore.

God's Little Instruction Book
God's Little Instruction Book II
God's Little Instruction Book for Mom
God's Little Instruction Book for Dad
God's Little Instruction Book for Graduates
God's Little Instruction Book for Students
God's Little Instruction Book for Kids
God's Little Instruction Book for the Workplace
God's Little Instruction Book — Special Gift Edition
God's Little Instruction Book Daily Calendar

P. O. Box 55388
Tulsa, OK 74155